Night Sweat

Nathan Leslie

H/s

Hamilton Stone Editions

Library of Congress Cataloging-in-Publication Data

Leslie, Nathan, 1972-
Night Sweat : poems / by Nathan Leslie.
    p. cm.
ISBN 978-0-9801786-2-3 (alk. paper)
I. Title.
PS3612.E78N54 2009
811'.6--dc22

                                    2009006076

H/s Hamilton Stone Editions
P.O. Box 43, Maplewood, New Jersey 07040

First Edition

Table of Contents

I.

Rain, Steam and Speed

The latest greatest claps through
morning mist, a wine bottle snake
riding a canoe bottom—sky smeared
with egg, water gauzy golden,
obsolete bridge pencil supports
in contrast to the bulwarks of new;
testament to the next newest,
iron locomotion clogged with
gawkers from the East and children
in their shiny Sunday best,
gold tassels on their sleeves.

Half concealed in shadow or steam
a boat nods far left, nosing away
towards the shallows downstream,
casting and reeling—consoling lovers
feeling the lap and tug of fleeting currents,
and as the train rushes past, the boat bobs,
shifting on each eddy in fading huffs—
wood, water and row—from the dusk
into the light of Turner's new age.

The Meat Stall

The head of a heifer,
half-skinned, nose still wet,
swine hooves, bowl of lard,
innards and sausage draped
over a barrel next to flanks,
a hogshead, fish and cocks
catty-cornered, skewered,
gashed, limp on wicker.

Three apertures beyond the flesh:
the prodigal son—hunched over
a well bucket, chain taut—pouring
into a jug, black and red surrounded
by clam shells and sand, the open air
mead behind, red-faced peasants frothing.

In the center the virgin hands alms
to a child, bowl outstretched,
line of faithful flanking them,
trees bowed for her passing,
and beneath the ill-used token,
a blue arbor, a path, a river
leading off, no man or woman in sight.

The Annunciation

From where she sits
upon a coffer
or useless stair—
Duccio's *Maesta Altar*—
the first glimpse
is the spiny head,
seven sprigs
of black tuber,
arm and hand
around the corner
from blackness
to the smolder
of her own halo,
enough to light
the room.

As she enters,
halo of her own—
pink robe,
gray underlay
and flaxen wings
fringed with emerald—
the virgin lifts
her languid arms,
glances ahead to
grasp the bulb.
She must,
faced with the open
Book in miniature,
words to Word.

The new orbital blush
reveals what the
crossed glances miss:
molding, converging
pyramid design under
the ceiling beams,
too short to stand,
and the curve of arches
leading only to night.

Arranged Wedding

In a time, in a place, I had nothing to do with it. It was a dream
       on silk.
I rode behind the lead horseman. The mahout tempered
the banner whipping his face and the stench of the horse and
       elephant
with a palm frond lashed to his head and a silken wrap over that.
I rode under the mahout's canopy, holding a cymbidium,
beads clipping my collarbones and rising again with each jostle.
The ox horn players blew one after another and carried scimitars,
and others carried more banners and held ornate shields,
and staves with banners attached to the poles,
and the flute player hummed behind me and played,
and others threw cymbidium flowers as we passed,
and others waved heliconias as we ambled by.
Behind them my wife in an ox drawn chaise
with a thatch canopy and musky curtains
to shield her from the sun. Behind her,
her ladies, wafting perfumes, carrying ointments for the night.
Behind them the rear guard, his scimitar tight in his sheath,
and behind him the litter of a desert too wide for us to cross,
and a chain of bald mountains, and in the distance
a lone swan floating in a lake, surrounded by tattered trees.
All of which I had nothing to do with.
And yet, as I craned my neck to see her, I detected
she held the same exact flower in the same position, and she
held her mouth the same way as mine, with the same
look of collapse as I imagined myself to betray.
I knew then we would eat the pollen if not the whole.

II.

Ada

6:05 lemon light and he clicks the door shut, bares himself,
slivering and downy under the sheets with me as ever.

His fingers burrow in my hair, twine my knotted nest—
the first sensation—and his leg hair
against my garish flesh,

and the whirl of his voice, the ridged underbelly
of his tongue grating the asphalt of mine,
and the knob of blood quickening
on me, filling and burrowing

into my thighs. And they part, and yes, lower.
Yes. I think of her and what she
must be doing at this moment,
sleeping, feeling the empty
spot, ignorant, hollow.

I possess complete liberty and few
pesky little obligations—to do,
or think, or act conjugal in a
certain way.
I can exist.
I am.

But I wonder if she knows or
suspects, or even if her soul
pings, scalding even now,
rending flesh, or
plotting plans
to meet
me?

Carney

Who knows if I could run the joint the way
I do now. If I owned it I'd make exceptions:
Someone *else* would jostle and chase
ganja punks from where they splintered the cues,
someone else would work from five to two
every weekend so *their* wife gives up and moves
back to her Jersey hometown in a huff,
and that someone else could learn how to angle
a two-nine combo for the county nine-ball win,
only to lose the set on slop shots and luck banks.

The punks must think I'm some washed up vet
dragging his duffel bag heart through the blue smoke.
Every year it's the same swagger, although we still
don't serve booze, and if you gamble you leave.
It's still the same strut, young gel-heads with
their too-tight-jeans-wearing-peroxide-skanks.
If the neighborhood cleanup committee wants to bust
crime, they'd put a stomp on swagger.

I go home and flip on the news and nurse
a long beer. I sit in the dark. Colors in rapid fire.
Around four I fall asleep, shaking it off like dandruff,
like dead skin, to the sound of TV gunfire and helicopter fuzz.

Chip

After the six figures, the laundry woman every Thursday,
the cleaning woman every Tuesday, the limo rides to and fro
the Regal and the Royal—these "important engagements"
with "important clients"—after working thirteen hour days,
shoveling lunch in a watch tick, there was self-exile
in Maine—lichen hikes in the shadows
of the Appalachians, the moss, the crusty lumps of snow
clumped around an oak root, a stump in the rain.

And after that, there was the little girl
who poured tea from the kettle
into the teacups so nothing spilled.
She didn't look at her teacher,
or even at me for glory or approval,
but to the fruit of her own labor,
and she offered the rest to her
classmates, if they wanted tea.

Then there were the Redwoods and the class—
my class. There was my mentor singing me,
forgetting the brush of paper in my fingers,
I watched, and let my fingers release,
and my blood pumped slower,
and my brain shuddered, stopped
when it could, if it could.

Donal

Instructions: Twenty hours post-mortem kindly
shave then skin the body head to feet.
Tan the hide, following given procedures.
Bind "Golgotha" in the skin of my torso.
Bind "Fescue" in the skin of my legs and feet.
Poetry for the ages.

Instructions: Deliver the volumes to Mr. Arthur Swanson
at the county library with given directives.
Remind him of our pact. Remind him he is under contract.
Allow students only in the enclosed room.
Someday fame? Someday posterity?

Instructions: Use the skin of my head, neck, arms
and genitals—hardened for the purpose
of binding my epic "The Stone Man."
This is to remain in your possession until
twenty years post-mortem. See above.
No bindings are to be dyed or discolored.
All bindings are to be treated with greatest care.
No photographs. No bare fingers. No pens or pencils.

James

Sitting shower with washcloth.
The silt of soap lather.
Wheel me to the table.
Let me sit in the sun.

On Sundays we drive.
Unless it rains, the park.
Unless the air is a vacuum.
We bring the box.

She sits me in a lawn chair.
I run the strings; she squints.
I watch the red and yellow whir.
She sits next to me in the clover.

This is my ordinary life up there.
The washcloth is a step away.
I can reach this from here.
Then the wind shifts.

The box topples and we jerk and tug.
The frame in one piece, send it up again.
She wheels me back to my spot in the sun.
I watch the ruts in the grass and squint myself.

Jerome

He tells me to hold the basin lip
as he heats it, the figure
of two horseshoes locked.
Entwined coat hanger.
Blow torch.
They clutch me again.
Calming, sweat, pat.
They slip the buckle,
shave any hair
on the spot
to draw a cleaner burn.

Then the hit. Crackle. Psssssst.
Seeeeearing sound.
Flesh blister. I'm tagged.

My great grandfather had this—
something like this—
on the same spot,
right flank, below the hip.
Those scar loops—
manacles to him.
For me not just a rite,
like all those frats do,
but a nod, a "Yes, I know."
A "Yes, I am blessed today."

My parents: "Do you think
you're a piece of meat?
Who says you're *owned*?"

But secretly they are bigheaded,
not the sacrifice—
minimal—
but the motion,
and the deliberation,
and the furtive part
underneath the ensemble
and silk lash.

Kristine

Hot gravel on my tender pink feet bottoms,
the bristles of dead Georgia grass, the glow
of new white tennis shoes in the dark
on fresh black parking lot pavement

all seem more important than when
some man's organ exactly enters
my organ on some balmy, breathy night—
lonely, filled with dense, sporadic din.

At 25 I play music with the bedroom door
ajar so my father can hear it, so he can become
an unwilling witness to my inner growth,
so he can track me back to high school pop,

and consider this progress—how now
I'll listen to gospel and blues—never
a thought before. This is how I thrive…a digression.
Concentrate on each moment, Kris, concentrate.

People think they are superior to me since
I'm not a beauty, and all the fat sticks
to my face, and I haven't fucked—
for Chrissakes—without reason.

But sometimes I get this blue dot of feeling,
a sudden sensation that events are askew
in a way, and I am stuck in a limited time,
in a limited place, in this raggedy skin,
and that I'm attached to something larger
that tugs me as a compass pulls the needle South.

Kurtis

If you place your finger
here you can feel it,
the back corner of it—
steel, yes, flash.
I dream in smells,
think in waves, white
bolts, dizzy and out.

I recall the monkey house,
the hippos, the stench—
our mouths were blue
from the stickiness,
and then, and then.

The nub is cool in
July and wobbles.
In January it reminds
me of chores, warms to
the touch of others
who pat my head,
brush the spot
on their way to my
forehead and crossed eyes.

Simon

My mother is calcifying into a hull of herself,
but who else sees her white hands, or her toes
aching from the weight of one scratchy sheet,
or how the catheter tubes and I.V. needles
make her seem like a starving porcupine?

I walk outside, try not to step on a single
insect, ant, mite, or spider. I am not a Sikh,
but I respect the frail intricacies, the accidental
patterns that have graced this world with geometry.
I bow to the sidewalk and touch the concrete

as if I were touching my toes in gym, as if I were
limbering before Wimbledon, and for some reason
HORSE comes to mind. I used to let my son win.
Now he is eighteen and blazes in fury, erupts.
And this is my doing. I created this. I have a stake in this,

and I can say many things without reproach, and I can say
to him, "I am sorry," and "I didn't mean to." My mother
will pass as we all will. Yet I can't stop myself from
throwing my own tantrums, telling them they must
do something—you must bring her out of this.

This is exactly what she likely felt at some
point, when I fell from the picnic table and bashed
my face against the ground, or fell from my bike,
and cried, and she didn't want to reach out to pick me up,
and yet she did, and then she walked away with me.

Stuart

We met when we were sprouts,
and I was the rangiest bud,
and she was a nubile spore muttering
through the early air, and she was drenched
in dew, and she was a stem of
a lily, and she was the lily itself,
and she was the pollen in the lily,
and the stamen, and the petals folding
into the morning glitter.

We fell into it first, and then that was my ache.
And then...and then what? The expanse
shrunk to a pinpoint, the sheathed mornings
became languorous afternoons, the languorous afternoons
became evenings, the evenings became nights, the nights
became the dusk of a new morning—yet it was not vital—
and the morning seemed identical to the first morning,
and the first morning seemed to be the only morning,
yet it wasn't, and it wouldn't be, and now what? Now what?

Then the chickens roamed the pen and we had to feed the
        chickens,
and tend the chickens, repair the hutch, prepare them
for being chickens, feed them more, care for them when they
        were
sickly, or upset, and support them if they were in need.
The morning, which was then an afternoon, became a chore.
Something to do, something to sweat over, something you
just endured, something you listed in your rotation of lists,
something to check off the slate and call done. And so it was.

III.

Five

My father and I play board
hockey on the three legged table,
on the nubbled sofa, peanut butter
and bananas, smell of refried beans.

With a switch of my thumb
a point, another blocked shot.
Final score: three to one,
though he let me win again.

I am in an Afghan nap when
the smell of onion and tomato,
melted cheese and tacos,
and a clank from the kitchen

rouses me. Filled with clouds.
I find a penny on the table
and whisk it into my pocket
without a sound, no remorse.

Nine

What it was: pebbles lobbed from the crag
above Main Street, chinking the windshields,
terns minus the swoop and flutter.

What it was: carving creek bed rubble into badges
among the discarded refrigerator, hub caps,
rusted beet cans, bottles of Beefeater.

Nine and two years past the hornet swarm,
a sham and stealth bid me from
wallpaper, pillows, whorls of spider webs.

Now lace my galoshes, roll up the cuffs:
flashlight through the drainage tunnel as
far as you can go, cursive, kiss and milk.

What it was: climbing the precipice over Main Street,
thist of pants against pants, reaching the pinnacle
and overlooking the hills, shops, gables, the steeples above.

Thirteen

She: headlights, ground glass
screen door, sump pump, mask
and hand in bag, roundness,
humus, shards of feldspar.

He: fists chapped, basement glow,
jump shot, high five, aluminum
siding, slap of leather and slide,
pitch the penny forward, win the spoils.

The sudden shift schemes
another: sentiment, memory,
and its opposite—prospect.
Yet, entering this dynamo today

I would tickle the same bones,
sift the same possibilities through the
fingers of my brain. Was the alley
from her to him too stark

(not in intention, but in weight
and blow)? And then what of
the end result—neither one—
both stranded on the jetty
in the sea of this sham practice?

Seventeen

I will grip the wheel
corner to corner,
hope he smiles.

Dig this hole,
stir the primer,
open this sash.

His eyes scamper at seventy
four, still climbing roofs
to check the tar.

We load the truck
and scramble to the next
house, inspecting furnaces.

His arm in an L,
painkillers in the afternoon.
Worn, I sleep to the July game crackle

and wake to the novelty
of a new, different place—
any escape will do.

Direction.
Clarity.
Purpose.

Three weeks of this though
and I'm back to
abstraction,

a coil in the brush,
pocketed behind each
action and reaction.

When will I *be*?
When can I find this
fleeting steadiness
without imposition?

Leave me alone.
Leave me alone.

One month and then
the openness, the void
of horizon.

IV.

Dishwashing

Before I'd see the scum
bobbing in rice froth,
fish scales, rye crust, and carrot peelings,
only hear the murky, tepid
water slosh in the basin and drain
with a squaaaaaawk,
and smell the oily lather filming
the belly of the basin and the dishes
themselves—never quite clean.
Before I'd only feel the toil of habit,
and disdain my twenty minutes away from
my "great moments" filled with "great ideas."

Now the spiny brush over a cheese grater,
or the polished plane of porcelain will
send an urge to blast more hot water,
squeeze more detergent and slip them all
with a blurp into the soapy heat.
I want to *know* my bowls and spoons.
Use is only part of care, and the machine
that we all want—can't do without—
dilutes intimacy in its rampage
of cycles and spouting jets of hot water
that smacks plates and knives,
that lashes glasses with soap
and rinse with calculation and speed.
But when you open the door
you can't remember where you put the peeler.

Aurum

The only way: Fireflies in mesh
bags strapped to feet, arms, head,
through ten miles of midnight morass
thick with chitters, black flies and adders,

across fields of rubble, scrap iron,
potsherd glass, sludge, bolts and
electrical wire—the only way to
a wide hollow, heavy with jagged

slabs of slate and siltstone where
the July deluge and land compact
to an annual tarn, lifting the sediment
from the bed and what could not

be divined without, and still the thought
of prior wings and talons of guillemots
and loons, grebes, and auks, found in
sharks and skates the size of kitchens

mediates this moment when we're at the murk
and all that's left is the contraband dive, only now
with batteries and bulb, for the Velazen
ingot (what they say lasts), and all this

to illustrate my merit—if she grants
me more than a sigh, and finds a method
to open a sluice, and allows the thick dregs
to sieve through and remain with her.

A Horse's Ditch

Riding her down to the river,
our dun Connemara tripped
over a stump in the moorlands.
Fourteen and thinned through
the Welsh Cob the commission
sought, trying to right the blood
on their blades—sending legions
of stallions from their west country.

With only words to go by,
and my common sense,
I know what was wrought
alone from these bogs will
never match some mixture
of foundation sires, set foot here
only to impart, just as the fen pony
and the Galloway were leeched
into the drainage—
knuckled ideas of Dutch engineers.

So we dig out a trench for
our shot-legged Connemara,
and we lead her in, glancing
from her dashing eyes
to deflect the pain of doing.
I put one through her skull,
and she crumples, head to soil.
We cover her over with the
slosh that caused her such
meddling grief at the start.

The Canal

Wide enough for two galleys
to pass, the canal of Darius
shimmered in the people who
laid claim to a certain
time in a certain space.
Yet, what was once center
becomes fringe as sands
shift, as tides yank the years:
Napoleon's dream was
stillborn to surveyors with
shoddy rulers; the queen's resurrected
canal brought her frankincense trees
from Punt, but silted as rains
drummed for centuries.
In the desert of navies
Cheops had pits to house sycamore
riverboats, still watertight in 1952.
Even now men and women blink
at the ring of his name,
point to the Suez proclaiming
amazement, raising the age
above their heads, as the sun
wends us around a whirlpool
with the mercy of a buzzard.

Fishing

The old men hold gourds
in their left hands as
they yank the lake
with scoop nets for red-eyed
tetras, the color of grass
tendrils shot through with sun.

They will grind the shoalers alive,
stone into stone, a paste
with cassava and rice and egg.
Fish all day for a pound.

Some cast spells, rubbing board
and root, others hex driving
nails into a spirit carving.
Can't do this always—luck's limit.

Watch them by the waters,
plucking prisms from
nets, thunking gourds
with the thrashing fish.

From Freon air
the water runs clear,
and all are smiles.

Glassware

Before she left this world,
she beckoned us each into her chamber
to offer pieces of her collection—
a dragon stem goblet for mother,
topaz wings, a Sarpaneva sculpture
blown in a burned wooden mould
for Anne, a lavender opaline
bell gilt with a bronze mount for me.
As for father—a cut glass
decanter with hobnail cutting,
a fluted neck ribbed.

As we loomed over her bed frame,
she spoke in throaty gasps,
skin bleary, eyes darkened with blood.
She recalled rumbling through prairies
as a child, nestling wildflowers behind
each ear, burning the stale brute chips.
We were thin, and yet she passed.

As I cradled my glass
close to my bosom,
I too shuddered at the sand
within it—just sand—so easily
swept up in a passing gust.

Bix at Sixteen

Rotgut and cornet in a paper bag—
ruffle my cords, see if I care.
Rip me from the waterfront so I can't
hear that woozy river music swell.
Expel me from Lake Forest—
throw me out, toss me into the pit,
banish booze under the threat of castration,
paint my hands black with dust
and call me nigger lover.
Preach me your Presby preach,
and garnish my bed with quilts and lace
surrounded by towers of Bibles and pine crosses.
Just don't take my cornet.
Don't take my Victrola.
Don't tell me he can't play,
and that his soul is not just equal,
but superior to mine—even if I can't
play with the man aside from hush-hush.
When I'm in your better place,
make sure you let that Dixie spin
over and over as I dream long and easy
and wash upon the shores of the lower Miss.

Jade After Frost

Ten plus, limbs splintered—
ice, water, snap—
drooped onto the rug,
elephant trunk bloated.
In from the porch cold,
rubbery ovals sodden,
dollops chilled to the touch.
I ask her why: "graceful exit,"
"old and ugly," "spatial effects."
A death sentence: out of desert
mountain rock meet nearing winter.
The bulk of this crafts the view—
so limb, so oval, so once and no longer.

Brothers

The summer before we mucked
knees and thighs glued to our trunks,
shrimp nets dredging the creek
with both hands, minnows and shrimp
commas among the shell shards
and silt. He held the pilings,
barnacles scraping knuckles,
red clay squish, queasy
at the thought of all beneath.
He'd hop out, climb the ladder
pier and scrape the boat side
for crabs or drop strings
of chicken necks, net quivering.
We'd row out to the cross-town
bridge, dangle worms
by concrete pillars, hope for
eels and sunfish. If we were
lucky he'd flatten one with an
oar and sling it to her for soup
and crackers, apples and cheese.
By November he was a glint,
an outline, a shimmer in mud.

The Firewatch

Up in mid-drift, swaying in
gusts, he hawks over the expanse
in a globe for the last glint or smolder.
This is a dry season of the heart.

Thoughts back to prism days,
her mouth without a purse,
the fulcrum of arms,
rotating fans, salt air, sailboat.

Boredom is the temptation,
thoughts lose their moorings
back to the horizon,
twenty-twenty plus some.

She's chemical, mineral,
a distant version.
Once was once,
and never still.

He sees a flash beneath
Kent's Knob, readies the call,
until the further glance
reveals only the sun's head.

Bookmobile

The janitor steers the horse-drawn
Concord through the back roads
of Washington County, words
on a cart, shelves propped
on blocks in the jostling rear.

The farmers and day labor
one-eye him, thumb through volumes,
mica chips dusting their foreheads.

The barterless exchange—borrow,
read, return in two weeks time
upon the route back through—
is the basis of May Titcomb's
vehicle, the library that arrives
like milk and paper news.

Yet, was it emancipation that
set forth the engine of this—
a means of conversion—
or an escape from wheat
and holes in the rocky soil?
A part of the whole,
eagles grasping for the upstart,
words to the continent
locking them out at once,
only to retreat from the window.

Two Car Garage

They must have dropped
in the middle of it all.
Mom held a glass of water,
the newspaper stretched on the table;
the young girl with a curling iron,
the radio blaring, mirror lights blazing;
the father in his sweatpants slumped over
the rowing machine, one hand still clutching
the rubber oar handle; and the son
head hinged over a stack of pillows,
the television on, remote control at his feet:
football game highlights, ads.

We walked through lightly, as though we might
wake them, and then we heard it:
the shimmer of the car engine in the garage,
attached, and I held a hand to my mask.
We walked into the carbon monoxide clouds
and cut the ignition, cut the radio static,
walked back through the living room,
kitchen, mudroom, bathrooms, upstairs, hoping
we wouldn't find another piece of this wax museum.
Not so lucky: Upstairs in the guest bed,
a woman slumped with a discreet smile on her face,
a small picture of a boy by her bed,
and next to that her alarm clock ticked
to wake her at four from an afternoon nap.

Burren

The check marked photo
tells me all I need to know:

Before the end she traveled five years past
to the limestone cliffs of Moher nearby.

But did she see the Burren—
yielding neither water nor land—

rounded whalebacks of limestone
dappled with clouds of yellow,

magenta and blue orchids, and the avens,
maidenhair ferns, and bloody cranesbill

from the rock heat, gnarled blackthorn
hoisting the grikes, turloughs vanishing

from sight when the water level drops
to the maze of caverns below?

Or the seventy tombs carved from the rock itself,
or the green road which runs below

the Slieve Elva away from the Caher overland,
rushing through the stone at Fanare and beyond?

The slender shelter grasses in the crevasses
on page one forty two answer yes.

So do the boulders lined with joints and cracks
strewn across the moon of the homeland.

v.

Beyond

How is this another color,
unseen beyond prisms?

How does this clutch
unknown specks?

Before you wake I
perch and watch

your breath in the
daybreak silence,

listen to the fall
of fog—

your lids flecked
by shadows

from the glass dew
and the rising light.

As I fumble out into
darkness, the hearth

of your touch still
smolders in

each step further,
sends tensile figures—

the dried tinsel of grass
as we first sat,

my face booked
between your hands,

the simple shiver
of your departing,

your thin fingers
on wrist bone hair—

ascending into crooks
of the darkness,

and I pinch and
clutch each

as they rise
and dissolve.

Attempting a word to
limn the gathering images,

and match the lushness
of my own sense—

a futile nod—
I stand silent still,

"love" scant for breadth,
depth or precision.

I return.
Darkness to light,

silence, breath,
the fog itself

ascending, the sun
buoyant beneath

the line of sycamores,
a whisk of daws.

I pass over you,
press against you,

burrow beneath
the heft of layers,

my return to the calm,
and blaze of your touch.

Raspberries

In thrashing nettles the bruise colored
berries emerge in patches on the gravel path
that runs behind my mother's house.

We walk through weeks early,
jolting rabbits from the weeds,
itching pastures overgrown for years.

The family left five rusted hills
in the boxwood yard and barns
pocked with rot and nesting birds.

The silo is fuzzed with ivy
and creepers, raspberries flanking,
sentries to empty threats.

As far back as I go we had tomatoes
and corn, a plot run through
with gravel as this, vultures hovering.

My father put a wheel in my hand
there—the pathway safe, straight,
direct, without curves or troughs.

Then raspberries lined the road as handouts,
offering themselves directly, gifts
for living, for breathing, solace.

Today, as we prod the clacking
doors with branches and squint
in the familiar sun, the fruited

thistles seem sharper, discreet,
less governed and clouds
darker, heavy with veiled turmoil.

The Summer Before

The summer before:
We drove in strands,
clustered in chills,
reeds venting past
miles of nozzles.

The summer before:
We ate in silence
staring at sky,
at spots on the wall—
within clamped eyelids.

The summer before:
We walked along waves,
we walked along streets,
we walked alone,
knowing without saying.

The summer before:
The storms drummed
and we watched the coast
and the horizon blaze,
the wind shivering our scalps.

The summer before:
We nested in sand,
we snapped to ourselves,
we counted dolphins,
hearing the sun fade.

The summer before:
We talked in pictures,
and listened in smells,
and tasted in words,
always slanted, awry.

The summer before:
We drove in strands.
clinging to relics,
the rain greasing us,
pounding without
thought or remorse.

Night Sweat

I still find shards of last
week's broken saucer
under the toaster, on the molding,
in the burner basket—ceramic sickles.

I doze in a half-sleep,
embarrassed at my old passions,
an abstraction from the warm
and breathing, a concept from myself—

a walking thought. A governing
principle lacking a scabbard is as
elusive as the all-encompassing
omniscience of my past—no longer

desired, no longer sparked. If only
talons, whiskers, udders and a mew—
a plow and hammer at the least.
Instead, the camera of my own

constant film spools through me
in steady streams. I dream
myself dabbing splinters,
a wet paper towel in limp air.

Yet this is sludged by my own
quickening, a thought into feat—
an occasion to strike out for
a widening sky, a road to standing up.

The Draw

The notice—approval for posting—
neurophysiological studies for siblings
of it: attention tests, eye movement,
memory studies, personal interviews.
I peel the flier from the floor tiles—
seared and dusted into size eleven—
and fold it into a windowpane
and into my chinos, and I'm on.

If not for cinnamon toast and
crimping pie shells, three inch
cardboard and aluminum sticks,
rook to A2, and her smile
into my Adam's Apple,
I could be the topic
of dissection and conduct.
The posting tape is an outlying scratch.

A meringue of calm mutes
the burble undetected.
The gut sharpness is contained
in an Easter basket;
plastic grass coils, a shield.
Yet, the sword is blade up,
interior and magnetic, a reverse
Excalibur honing a rock draw.

Balance

Between two in tatters
is the natural state
for a mountain goat,

a swimmer of central
currents, a walker
of balance beams.

But is this sway
the parking lot
for a determined pitch,

or a limb for leaves
teetering on the brink
of a final plummet?

They ask me, glasses
clinking to the glaze
of olives and brie:

Why do you tether
lines, afflict words
into fixed contortions?

I cough and peer towards
poppies or the cat's swish.
But now the balance bleats,

casts shafts upon the point:
to keep my hands
hard and waggling,

eyes directed parallel
to miss the fall
myself, a fly's halter.

Guidance

Their conception of failure
is the failure:

metaphysics kneeling to
a microscope, a Benz,

the literal taken literally,
the irony of the loss,

a finial on a lake bed,
Scotch at death.

The effect—a retreat
to the manifest sources:

wounds on a palm,
the lines of type.

Who has obliged a grape
dangling over our mouths?

When will the crisp fringes
of volition reveals themselves?

Answers point to context,
yet the spirit is hushed

and shudders under the weight
of its own sleepy skin.

Horizon

What is it for scope, for the horizon
without the craggy shadows of brush,
or horse, or spruce appendages
jangling in the airstream of this horizontal
vacuum? A mop for the huddle
within this daily lattice? A reverie reversal
of this mind's squiggled incest?
A paint thinner for breath and Lao Tzu's
alleviation (if only—the simple pastille)?

For months peanut butter and wheat
gummed my linings in the name of
this sigh, countless days trodding
through thickets and groves for the
brambles to unwrap grass and firmament.
Now the sun amplifies, and the salt and froth
shrug towards this need. But for umbrellas,
and the screech of two-legged crabs.

Within the smolder of illumination
and the ginger undergarments of exchange,
this horizon is now under the lids
if not in the blasts and wrath of ferment
that razes solitary vigor in howling squalls.
Yet sleep slips easy and the pillow,
for now, is sere and brittle.

Hands

Imagine: This is not an epiphany,
but the opposite—a being
stretched to the point
of disbelief, where his
own extinction shaded
beneath his eyes, augured
in a duck of his head,
a glance away, fingers
blinking in edgy spats,
hands clutching themselves.
Still, the lacquer widened,
since the out was always
easier than the thorny in.
Our one and only.

There are some whom calamity
hovers over, whose silhouette
casts murky. We consider this
a solace. Still, this sorrow's
vibrancy was only the first
tug upon us, a launch into
the liberty within him that incited
this—the menacing, the looming.

In his rank flat we opened drawers,
packed boxes, rifled papers
and packed redundant spoils—
another microwave and toaster?
Still, the smell, the purple odor.

Then he found the trunk tucked within
the closet, and now I wish my hands
had clasped his and hurled
it far from us. Instead, a crowbar,
and inside dim fingers, wrists, gluey rags
of flesh, in hundreds, hands
like sodden crab cadavers clustering
for warmth on a primeval sea bed.

VI.

The First Emperor

If the mandate is exact,
we must bolster our ramparts.

Forgetting the long pagan slide—
Alexandria, the empires of the sun,
the first emperor was not the first.

The millet growers learned erasure,
as Shih Huang Ti revolved beds under
the spell of Fang Shih demon hunters.
I am the first, the only; swab your foreheads

of the Chou, the Shangs, the T'ang's mulberry grove.
Scholars nook Confucius in clay blocks
and rabbit holes only to fall
four sixty flat. Tyranny is found ready
in how it holds a frame, or gashes a
canvass, bulldozes marble, lights parchment.

In red, white and blue we sing
the anthem in bleachers, nestle into wide-
screen, stare into glowing boxes.
Yes, marble is just a stone, and watercolors
only for first grade. When the aging
dynasty shows its cracks the millet
farmer will fail to see the dust storm whirl.

Imperial Palace

The white plaster cracks
from the bottom up,
a broken straw.

The iron clasps meet,
two lower case
tees,

horseshoe ends rising,
a capital H—

mustached
when closed.

Where the door
parts, a gash
bleeding

in between buckles
upright.

A dollop scar to
the left

holds it,
a crescent
to the right

to solicit, muffle,
and condemn.

Above it all a mere
blush,
scuffing the face
like a halo.

A Mild Disruption

On a Mondrian grid
of sidewalk a man
in an overcoat stands,
umbrella canted to the right.

The sidewalk is complete
precision, aside from the slight
disjoint of parts where
the perfect squares miss.

Tickets and scraps of paper
litter the blocks, and moisture
throws the man's shadow to
a blur on them. A lone
can rolls along the convergence.

Relics

Don't take this wrong:
Miracles are miracles.
It's only the design

of queuing for a knuckle
bone that puts me off,
not the end result—

if you can believe tales
of dud eyes wiped clean,
and hard ears that perk to jingles.

Picking my poison,
I'll take the route littered
with deliberate prayer

rather than bazaar ends
imported from Ireland,
Lisieux, or some such.

If I told Therese that a saint's
scalp might help her cause,
would she falter on her course

to die a solid death, to seal
her bones into the lining of
time with a nod and a sigh?

Carving

You can breathe through burlap
but the husks
at the back of your throat,
and the dull breath
stifle nose to mouth.

A chisel, granite bulks,
driftwood: These alone would
rally my spores
twenty years back.

Now a faint campus posting
culls motes.
Ideas sag or loiter,
and what was once fresh
seems barren.

I recall the flash of bulbs,
scents of paint and roses,
wine corks bursting,
pedestals plated with gold.

The afterglow seeped north
like kudzu leeching
life from branches that once
carved lions and serpents
from His dust.

The Noble Art

I'll dash off a glib one using "zither"
as the sun rises, or an index
of sensations each with stanzas
of twelve syllables but the last.

Yet, at my casual lunch,
the modern sublime annexes
this thought—stormtroopers
into the limpid Alps.

Notes singe with the insistence
of a blade against lithe pulp—
a compression that no fusion
of glyphs or missives can share.

The vain trail of a trumpet,
the simple shish of cymbals
can, without exertion, outstrip
the labor of a scribbled season.

Yet I am fastened by this blunt
gratuity, and after tea and the flip
of lean paper I'm within the lines,
throbbing to stir logic to make heart.

Kandinsky at his Easel

It already exists on the canvas.
I only have to find it.

Rembrandt's knobby faces float
in my eye, but not as faces.

The concealed colors in pink,
in black tassels and silk—just layers—

yet layers that lure
and hide simultaneously.

The object?
Dissolved in color.

The cheek is only a blend
interchangeable with silk.

Without the cheek—then what?
What replaces the object?

For now—the humming canvas,
waiting for my recollection.

Concentrate. Color.
Concentration. Texture.

The colors hiss
as they blend.

I am replicating Genesis,
only not yet.

No need for models lunging
breasts and thighs at me.

With a dash of memory,
no need for mimicry.

I listen,
wait.

I am an upside down
beetle grasping for a grass blade.

This tree trunk makes the
branch possible as I'm

waiting for the canvas
to grow the branch.

The object is steeped with
spirit, another gauze.

There, I know.
Color chars me.

I see bursts,
not the line.

My brush takes me
into it,

the whiteness,
then the stroke.

Travelers Among Mountains and Streams

That he allowed a name
is enough. The thin egress
from the crevice, the spruce
shards appearing in relief
against the bulk, the gnarled
trunks in counterpoint to the
vertical thrust—all stunted
by the cluster of sheer
rock, sprayed with sun,
capped by brush stubble,
and fringed by the haze
of waterfall and stream.
Underneath, the thread
of horses and men upon the road
seems sparse, reedy, and as
slight as soot within
the kiln of the gods.

The Portrait

The stain of light from
the thick, entrenched hole
reveals a woman in a sable,
pearls and earrings to her neck,
hair black as her husband
standing stiff next to her.

Their picture is aslant,
strung up on thick thread,
yet the tattered bristles at the
window deny them the moment,
curling the shopworn into redundancy.

Billboards

snarl around him
in his thinker pose,
in the sand and scruff,

scabs

of cardboard and wrappers
in patchy weeds,

barefoot.
A man in a fedora walks away
behind the Atlantic Ale
and Beer. Full of Good Cheer.

Above The Average
the Better 2 for 5 Cent Cigar
Phillies.
Tampa Nugget.
Royal Crown Cola.
Old-Union Bottle Beer. 7up.

The man above him
stables a tray of bottles
and glasses with both hands,

teeth white
and wide as his shirt cuffs.

Abutting the rear plank board shack,
a gas tank rusts next
to a greasy black bag.

Column and Tire

The sweep of human testimony contained
in West Palm Beach, 1941:

a cracked stucco wall, the slats of a vent
framed on the left by a wobbly
telephone pole pared
to its tree carcass,

edged by dusty pebbles,
the sallow rubble
of bone ash, death fusing
a backdrop.

In the forefront a tire leans,
its white rim
grimed to gray,
scored in two notches of tread,

the base a scoured remains of a column,
Corinthian thicket mounting
to a hewn head.

Tottering
on the rim, the bleached and
whittled remains of a whelk armors
this barren blind alley

to what may sweep across
this desert, as each did before.

Mother and Child

Face to breast,
his forehead cupped
at the nipple,
ear a wedge of pepper,
body furled in white.

Underneath.

A black comb
toothed in her hair,
her eyes sink to him
with an impacted smile.

But not exactly.

She never makes
it that far down.

A paisley and leaf
blueprint
sketches the silhouette
of her body.

The Match

Here is an image of him,
an image of her.

He salutes a waterfall,
she's prostrate in grass.

Coil them in separate tubes,
and dismember, mix

with pulverized stone and sweetgum,
place the two piles in the vase,

bounded with seven twigs.
Bury this in a hearth.

Ignite a plume, and let it run.
Place ice within the fire.

When it has melted, dig the vase,
plaster the heated remains in amulets

with the legs of beetles,
and spiders and bits of shell.

This is how they will fall in love,
and how you make it so.

Talk

In early May the leaves
are arrow points, windblown,
metallic and incandescent jade.
The lake pavilion
moans from ceaseless
gusts and beech branches
grate against the roof,
the tattling scrape of bark
and tin, a constant chatter.

Tomorrow we will
sit on chairs, on cushions,
sipping tea and reading
for hours. We will touch
without speaking, glances
laden with pages of acumen,
embedded within roots,
webs, knots, a complex
of sense—icebergs, carrot tufts.

On slanted sofas of lamplight
they hear words, judgments
furrowed in tulle, impressed,
crystallized in neon.
They recall, blowing within
a jagged fence, words
etching the line forward
onto a horizon of the same—
words to sounds to grunts.

But as I sit beneath the raking,
a cardinal flutters to perch
on the railing, then another.
Their heads pivot, feathers
hinged in the wind.
The need for calls stunts
against the closeness,
and the circle within
and without, ringing regardless.

The Rift

Anticipating the biting drone,
I rise at four sixteen,
snap off the aborted alarm
and step into the blackness.
The mid-November chill impels me
to the coat closet; with a tremor I scout
the horizon and eastern sky toward
Jupiter where the paper claims
the Leonids will dart and stream

from the Lion's head for hours.
Then flashes. I surge back into the house,
wake her and quickly exit, her hand
in mine, afraid for a blank slate.
We slump beneath a maple
near the bike trail, not alone—
the lamped shadows of a couple
a football field away chain smoke.
The sky is banded with red and green

and white, dust to slivers
of color every second;
rising to sparks, sitting is thorny.
Then, for a moment, I grasp the basis
of empires, how notched
bones and cairn spider webs,
astrolabes and horizon towers pined
after seasons, a glimpse of future,
Sirus to blare a month of planting.

Still, the Spanish undercut the
Ushnus for mountain aqueducts, spearing
a flag of advance to Times Square until
we view their very towers as puzzled rubble:
"They must have been so terrified at the
Leonids," or "they imagined they were
the dead, foreshadowing the apocalypse."
Millions have viewed this before,
and still millions will—yet who

could proclaim the familiar a scarcity,
and distill knowledge to creaky gears?
More likely: Rather than a blurb
in newsprint, the sky scores and stony
circles bore the specks of texture—
the symbol it wound through
a clustered polygon of views that
processed the shower within its own
pinpoints and shapes towards the whole.

We hold hands under the display,
and huddle against the frost,
speak in gated, almost courtly
murmurs—for this is once only.
Our testimony has crafted something other
than glass crescents: eyes without
vision, iotas that lead to oohs,
lenses rather than ciphers,
and heat and tea only a breath away.

VII.

The Shallows

In the shallows at high tide
they crease the sand,
and kneel in the sun-warmed
water, splashing with buckets

or cupped hands and running
barefoot, limp-haired, beaming
through the back current,
a miniature torrent to the sea.

Twenty odd years later, seated
on a paint-flecked bench,
I wonder how their parents
so easily release them into the froth.

In 1816 3,500 bound slaves found
their throats cut at the death
of an Ashanti Queen—old age—
sashes and shells glazed in blood.

A nameless artist cocoons
bicycle wheels, typewriters, soda cans
in yellow and orange and blue yarn
to sell or give away.

The phone call to the gas
company is more common,
but kin to these, a poke
in the eye, a clutch of fingers.

Away from it, the shallows,
two weeks vacation,
a startled glance at a patch
of woods on the commute home,

and the glimmer of light
on water, the residue of sand sparks
a glance further—a narrow grant,
something close to perfection.

A Fishing Poem

At five I snagged a three pound bass
on a miscast into the reeds.
But that was my peak.
On a boat in the Severn we caught
eels, crabs, bluegills, croakers.
When he bashed a hooked bluegill
with the butt of an oar
I had to look away.
The crabs clawed at the kitchen pot
as the water bubbled to a boil.

Poets craft gauzy lines:
fly fishing in the Missouri,
paddling out to a rock
in Lake Superior,
bobbers dancing in eddies,
worms dangling in crystal waters,
the men silent, stoic—a salty, mythic bond.

My young cousin reads her
textbook. She cocks her head, asks me:
"What does vestigial mean?"
I grab a bag from the freezer,
nod us to the creek.
We walk down the mossy stairs—
to the dock, the air ripe
with tar and moldering wood.
The creek is gray with effluence,
and fish float belly up

bobbing on the rainbow crests
of motorboats. I open the bag,
grasp heads and tails,
the eyeballs and crimson guts,
toss the chum into the creek,
and then I point. Blood sputum:
all this in the end.

On Rocky Gorge Reservoir

Embarrassed by defeat,
I kayak with my father.
The Rocky Gorge Reservoir
is narrow, unraveling across
the county like an orange peel.

The hefty terrapin ducks
into the water from his sunning
log, and herons swoop
across the far bank.

I startle a huffy mother
and her fawns in the shade
of a pine grove. My father's
arms ache and he sips water
warm from a plastic bottle
yards back; I explore.

In a cove I spot a bobbing
gray-blue body, a decayed flour
sack shape. The water is smooth
as I row myself closer.

The brown paddle tail gives
it away, face down
in the brown water.
Coke and Miller bottles line the shore.
Butterflies, wings firm, feast

on the rotting back flesh
and wet flank of the beaver.
I crane my head as I pass,
rubbernecking, then avert

my eyes. My father bobs silently
along the middle of the reservoir,
head down, shading his face
from the glare with his hand
held at a cockeyed angle.

The Creek

For how many years
was the culvert a dump?
My sister and I found
washing machines, tires,
rusted box springs, hordes
of brown bottles, beer cans.
Location, location: The creek
abuts a parking lot. Easy
access, easy.

At seven my friend Kevin
said we should bust an old jar
of peanut butter with rocks.
How were we to know
hornets made it their home?
Dashing across the planks,
we were stung by something
close to hubris.

Thirty years later,
on the way to my mother's
I pulled into the lot,
dashed across the planks
into the woods by the creek,
and pissed against a mossy rock.
How quickly youth evaporates.

Black Vulture

No mere devil, he is reborn with square tail,
bare head of skin,
neck black,
white patch of undersurface at the wing base.
Rapid flaps,
then a long glide,
eying a carcass from the tips of primeval trees,
not swooping,
dropping
to feast, to bark, to hiss and grunt, wings swollen,
slathering over
the she-vultures,
blood-beaked, strutting, entrails pink on asphalt.
Jim Crow,
John Crow,
black buzzard, bad news, come north to Hinkley,
to ledges
on lakes.
Watch out herons, lambs, skunks, turtles, slaughterhouses,
city dumps,
road kill.
In March the ominous light of August comes to roost,
eyeing toddlers,
shadows carving
fields up the basin and east, from Yoknapatawpa
to fetid waters
to lunch
among turkey vultures, to be one among the flock.

Wrentit

Though I hiked the juniper
trails—spying lizards, coyotes,
hares and hawks—I never
saw the sphere of feathers
ringing its whistle in the chaparral.
I never saw it trilling
to its mate, plucking toyon berries,
wasps and caterpillars from branches
like a crochet needle into its hash.

We can live a life without
so much. The clouds pulse,
and steam rises and falls,
and our small cycles remain.
My mind spiders to a thousand
options and settles from exhaustion.
They say the wrentit is the only
bird living solely here,
perched on a two acre spot,
content within its habit.

If she breaks a wing you can
palm her into a shoebox, finger
boiled eggs, cherries and hamburger
into her mouth, a momentary rest.
Healed, the brown ball will stiffen,
firm into a W, perk and lift
into unseen places beyond
the blue hills, homeward bound.

Bohemian Waxwing

Dart and dash like a band of gypsies,
fall and winter, twittering in cinnamon
and chestnut. Catch dragonflies in midair.
Summer: Turn to chokecherries, rotten apples.
Nest in tamarack, in open muskegs.
Hoard grasses, lindens lined with moss.
Cheep in zips, and if there's time
alight upon my shoulder, anoint me.

All is Food

Aside from concrete and stone, all is food.
Watch a hog root, a crow swoop for food.

The trees, the grass, soil, water, dung
are for something or someone the right food.

Pythagoras was onto something; but would you
rather have the number eight or food?

In Quebec City: Crepes three meals a day;
I dream of farfalle, quenelle and spiced food.

I make a mess: mulligan stew, baking bread, pies.
Time to learn nan and pot stickers, Greek food.

Once, my fat roommate would make ratatouille,
simmering tomatoes and eggplant, health food.

The calm of chowder, of lasagna and basmati rice;
eating or making or smelling—all is food.

Eat satays and ragout, gnocchi and bisque;
someday arthropods and beetles will digest us, food.

For now, how often can we forget our names
in the scents and textures, in the beauty of food?

Through the Desert

On my first glimpse I was swelled by the desert,
the cusp of the South Dakota Badlands desert.

I drove to Colorado to the desiccated plateaus,
the nettled yellow plains and sand duned desert.

In Utah I slept for weeks on red clay,
perched on the edge of escarpments and butte desert.

As the sun drained, the sky opened to distant storms,
seen across the broad pan of red desert.

Closing my eyes, I walk Arizona feasting on succulents,
on lizards and the juniper berries of the desert.

I panic musty javelina and mule deer through
the saguaro and ocotillo and mesquite desert.

I fly to San Diego and trek the Mojave, singing
to the sand verbenas of the Joshua Tree Desert.

You can live in a yurt or a Hogan or a tent,
join the Bindibu or Bushmen, rooting in the desert.

You can herd yaks in the Gobi, or dig crators
with the Matmata in the cool night of the desert.

You can hunt ostrich in the heat of the Kalahari,
hoard water in shells, burying them in the desert.

The pull is palpable when you open your eyes.
My furtive name is Sand Reed, lover of the desert.

Ars Prosetica

For stimulation, the grout and tile, the fencepost, the hedge trimmings, the clickings of cardinals in elms. This is the life Flaubert advised. I comb newspaper clippings, *News of the Weird*, gossip, tabloids, trivia. When business men on fire fling themselves from skyscrapers, words don't resonate; they coagulate. A movement by Mahler seems emaciated. Cezanne is superfluous.

Shall I eat a peach? Shall I observe pastiche? Shall I climb Kilimanjaro?

I scribble notes in some antiquarian mimicry of the illustrious dead. As if this isn't redundant. As if anybody reads. As if words carry more than their mere ink.

It is the best of times, it is the worst of times. A mystery of vast proportions. All that in a kilobyte.

For stimulation, the curtains in the breeze, an approaching hailstorm, moldering azalea blossoms. Then after that, a walk. Connectives. Scribbles in a composition book. Distributed by Blackhawk LLC, Pleasanton, CA. 94538. 100 sheet. Wide rule. And an audience: me myself and I. Then repeat all over again.

The Prize Winner

Your poetry writes biographies
of water, runs sans title,
black rimmed,
weighs meaningful   gaps
        spaces   designed
to   proffer   a
        sense
                            of
    depth   beyond   words.

Your poetry is for an audience
of exactly one, scribbled
while smoking cloves to the nub,
wearing merlot red thrift store sweaters
over pleated Prada skirts,
while eating fifty dollar vegan dinners.
Your poetry strikes glamorous poses.
Your poetry gapes into the camera.
Your poetry is, like, so Other.
If the lines exceed our understanding,
they must wield depth.

Colons: these: set: ideas:
in motion, like blurbs, like MFAs
from Iowa, Columbia, like abstract, puke green
pseudo-Rothko, rectangled covers, like: colons.
No need for titles. No need for readers—
readers are bourgeois—
when a: Punctuation mark says it all, as if you
invented the: colon.

What the body offers the room (2)
      are staggered lines,
            is the word
    leaf.
Nature glimmers:
like   nothingness
      the exact sum
           your book: offers.

An Old German Couple

They are coarse smiles
removed from
the road, the storm
drain, the camera lens.

White parcel under one
arm, tie, white collar,
top hat, all black:
He is Mr. Monopoly—

great man of industry,
a fossil, wedged ears,
smooth fabric and craggy
visage in morning light.

At home: lace, embroidery,
ancestral gilded picture
frames, rugs from
a lost edge of Prussia.

His wife's stockings
are black even. Her eyes
spangle, as if she knows
what they are made for,
how exactly they fit.

Watching Charlotte

At six months
she nudges
herself along
the carpet—
neck muscles, head,
a reverse inchworm
balding her means
of transportation.

When ice etches
through my veins,
she will
yawn and blink,
drink coffee,
make love,
listen to Brahms
at dusk.

From fish
to chicken
to human,
her eyes will
click from blue
to gray
to brown.
Soon she will set
solid;
she will remember
herself.

The Tomboy

Shoots skeet, chews chaw, lifts barbells
each morning before work, alone.
And later she plays ball—
cursing, stomping, pushing, spitting.

I watch her, envious.
My mother, I think. My husband.
I fill expectations, cook and clean,
dress in Laura Ashley prints.

I'd like to step her way,
grab it by the horns—
but for the price;
but for the zinging eyes.

If I'm lucky she will babysit
Johnny, Jordan, Caitlin
when the moon dangles from clouds
like a pendant, an ancestral stone.

I will sashay in diamonds,
Tim on my arm,
offer my blessings, a smile,
my manicured fingers clicking

our engraved brass doorknob.
She married a burly man, likes the security.
She has wings, dances naked
in the moon, bathes in bubbles,
blasting reggae for men who
knock at her invitation, slide in the glass.

Scales

When her husband's paramour died
in a winter plane
crash

she marveled at the extent
of his mourning, his eyes
cloudy, thumbnails torn.

He stabbed at the ground
hoping to bury a jade earring
in the frozen soil.

Which force is greater: pity
or envy? A grocer of grief,
she weighed each one.

Could she retain the jealousy
due her when the object
was in particles? Could she refrain

from spiking a heel into the same
ground come spring when the freeze
leached into soil, rock and root?

Her husband's gaze didn't offer
assistance; she came to see his eyes
as no longer hers, his stare in particles.

Faith

If you want to know why I stick to the pew
while the rest kneel for communion,

or why I skip the viewings, the wakes,
the baptisms; if you would like insight

into the distaste in the back
of my throat, it begins with a notion.

Digging spurs into the soft flesh of ambiguity:
As he said, faith is a flight from truth.

Our friend slept in the basement
for two years—a consequence of disbelief.

How many bleed on the street?
How many lie shackled in the dark,

gnawing on cockroaches, shitting in the corner,
a sacrificial lamb of some imperceptible mark?

In the Rumpus Room

We eat raw bok choy and crack Brazil nuts,
lift demijohns of steaming froth
and cruets lined with oily residue.
If I told you I am a coxswain,
an organ grinder, would you still
find me disarming? Would you dredge
the lake for my body if I went missing?
Listen to the accordion music.
Find the mallard decoys, the ibex statuettes.
Avoid boilerplate, driftwood chochkies, prospectors.
Listen to the Norfolk pines, the cowbirds in them.
The lattice frames your figure, cuts it into a bite-sized grid.
If we live as long as we should, hold my poncho,
indulge my crewel embroidery and stuffed ocelot,
allow me to fret the foreclosure red tape, for now.
We can hide in the rumpus room,
listen to the shrikes. The officials will knock,
wearing azurite; pray they don't find us.
Promise me the forceps aren't rusty,
that you can pinch me at arm's length.
Pinch me awake when the clouds cover the sun.

In the Shade

Twenty cicadas encrust our mailbox pole,
and I sit on the patio watching
a turtle lumber through
the grass, thinking of your touch.

I wanted to write a poem
about the nature of time,
of grace, or the essence
of fury in a lost world,

but whirling blades whine
through the trees, and the snow peas
we planted and the oily feathers
of the grackles pecking the grass

tell me this will do. Behind our house
winter creeper slinks from elms;
the shade casts a haven.
What else is there?

The Lake

*"No servitude is more disgraceful
than that which is self-imposed."* —*Seneca*

In the cabin by Luey Lake
we listen to the water lap
the shore as we sleep.

I dream of dragons in the foothills,
of my son's smile—though I'm no father—
of a pure feeling of exposure

as the doors clack unlocked,
a rush of risk meshed
within this, waiting for a story.

This sanctuary for a week
is the lake itself—the island
in it and the mere rock

in Indian Lake dotted with wildflowers,
moss, lichen, scrub bushes and beetles—
not merely in the mind, a thought.

His dashboard yellow sticky note proclaims
that he is "pure consciousness,"
visible as a sigh, tangible as breath.

Not only a shock of pain,
but the incline above us claims
otherwise: Whether or not I dream

the mountain rises and erodes,
the streams widen and oxbow,
the birds die and harvest.

Ten millennia from now, who will
sit in this desert, scratching over this skull,
this chunk of granite?

Dream Twenty-One

The park is only open on Tuesdays.
I hike down into the gulch,
through moss, grass and lindens.

As the land gives way to rubble
on the far side of the gorge,
I shrug, walk on distant treetops.

The clouds are gauzy
up close and wings flap
about me. Smells fade.

My people live up here,
nested in the upper reaches—
a yard of sky.

I cook potatoes and steaks,
and we eat on the deck,
we breathe in gulps.

Their child is new to me,
a bundle on backs,
a gasp of vigor.

Two feathered knobs jut
from his back. They warm each
with palms and tongues.

They bend over his mouth,
and offer him the vomit
of their inner cheeks.

"One day," they say. "One day."
They smile, rosy, unbidden.
It will be done.

They always were ambitious,
I think, and shrug—
it's lonely in the boughs.

Amid the thunder I slide down
the trunk five hundred feet;
under falling needles I walk home.

Orbit

Red starburst in neon, road humped
in viaducts and cracked double lines:
I drive on, your hair seething
in the wind, and you sleep.
My stomach snarls; I consider
turning back, but don't.
We'd like to make our mark,
I think. This tablet land.

Red starburst in neon, humped road,
ivy strewn viaduct, cracked lines:
You mumble; I close the window.
"Your faith in me is damp,"
you said once; I watch your lids
twitter. You are my eternal host.

Red starburst, neon, road in humps.
Crumbling viaduct, lines cleaved:
What I would give for a sign.
My cheek droops to my chin.
You turn your back to me,
a billboard. I'd like to,
but I must drive.
Where are we going?

Neon, red, bursting, humps,
mound of stones, phantom lines:
You leach into the seat, a stain,
a wake of worming hair strands.
I tried to tell you I'm helpless,
a missile in full orbit: love elsewhere.

Acknowledgements

Thanks to the magazines that originally published these poems.

Adirondack Review: "Seventeen"
The Amherst Review: "Nine," "Aurum" and "Rain, Steam and Speed"
Amoskeag: "All is Food"
Artemis: "Brothers" and "Jade After Frost"
Bluesap: "The Canal"
Comstock Review: "Orbit" and "Watching Charlotte"
Connections: "Carney"
Daybreak: "Arranged Wedding"
Driftwood: "Scales"
Edgz: "Donal"
Ekphrasis: "Burren" and "The Meat Stall"
Facets: "Ada," "Two Car Garage" and "Bix at Sixteen"
Fairfield Review: "Fishing"
Freshwater: "Relics"
Gin Bender: "Travelers over Mountains and Streams"
Harp Strings: "A Horse's Ditch"
Illya's Honey: "Annunciation"
Manorborn: "Mother and Child"
New Zoo Poetry Review: "The Match"
Northern Virginia Review: "Glassware" and "Kandinsky at his Easel"
Peshekee River Poetry: "Thirteen"
Pittsburgh Post-Gazette: "Dishwashing"
The Poetry Motel: "Jerome"
Quercus Review: "Five"
Rearview Quarterly: "A Mild Disruption"
Red Hawk Review: "Faith"
Red River Review: "Simon" and "Chip"
Saranac Review: "The Shallows"
Sea Change: "Night Sweat"
Southern Indiana Review: "Kristine"
Story South: "Raspberries"
Tamafyrh Mountain Poetry: "Kurtis"
Vallum: "Black Vulture"
Ward 6 Review: "Ars Prosetica"
Yawp: "The Firewatch"

www.ingramcontent.com/pod-product-compliance
Lightning Source LLC
Chambersburg PA
CBHW051814040426
42446CB00007B/665